APRICITY AND STARDUST

A POETRY ANTHOLOGY

SAKSHI AGRAWAL

Made with ♥ on the Notion Press Platform
www.notionpress.com

For Akshay, my husband

Thank you for your humour, kindness, and patience.

You light up my world.

Contents

Contents

Preface

Apricity & Stardust loosely translates to warmth and magic, which is how I view poetry. This book is a collection of poems centred around the themes of love, kindness, hope, grief, dreams, nostalgia, and womanhood.

I belong to a family of avid readers, where I was introduced to the joys of reading at a very young age- whether it was an insightful newspaper article, a wholesome poem, a heart-wrenching book, or a hilarious comic strip- I grew up with a deep understanding of what a great privilege it was to read something good.

And ever since I can remember, I wanted to contribute to this enchanting world of words. I yearned to craft my own magic. So, I started mentally noting the lines that resonated with me. I paid attention to the flow of words, the power of emotions, the impact of facts, the diligence of the writer. I started reproducing my version of reality on paper. And that's how my journey of writing began- by mimicking, trying, learning, and persisting.

Poetry has been a saviour for me there by my side through all my highs and lows, my successes and failures, my heartbreaks and achievements. Poetry has been a safe space for me, my anchor and my launchpad. And through this book, I bring to you a slice of that delight. If you love reading, I hope this book feels like a warm embrace. If you love writing, I hope you connect with the emotions woven into my poems. And if you are seeking inspiration, I hope this book helps you get over your creative block and gives you the spark you need.

Apricity & Stardust is all the times I woke up in the middle of the night, because I had just thought of a good line. It's a summary of all the notes that my phone is filled with. It's the child of my imagination and experiences, a fragment of everything that I am and aspire to be.

This is my debut book and I bring it to you with lots of love. May the poems bring warmth and magic to your life, just as they have brought to mine. May you get as much joy in reading the book as I did in writing it.

Acknowledgements

Everything I have achieved so far, I owe it all to my parents. In a middle-class family of a small town (Bhagalpur in Bihar), they ensured that I always got the best of education and the best of platforms to hone my skills. I am eternally thankful to you, Maa and Papa, for being my biggest cheerleaders, for giving me the courage to dream big, and for clapping the loudest when I achieved my dreams.

'The day you saw the world for the first time, was the day I was alone for the last.' Thank you, Siddharth, my baby brother, for believing in me when nobody else does and for lifting me up after every stumble.

I have been lucky many times, but most of all, when I got married. Thank you Mom, Dad, and Parul for rejoicing in every good news I share, applauding every achievement of mine, and always being such a staunch support.

The best thing that has happened to me lately is meeting Akshay. Thank you for saying, 'We are a team', and meaning it every single day since we have been together. Also, special thanks for designing the amazing book cover and helping me with the edits (which never seemed to be enough, no matter how many times we revisited the contents).

I am thankful to the faculty and environment at my alma mater, Mount Assisi School in Bhagalpur, for fostering the holistic growth of students. Rev Fr Joselet Chakalakal and Late Sir D. Banerjee were my mentors, who recognized my writing skills early on in school and continuously pushed me to perform better.

Many people have appreciated my writing along the way, and their words have amplified my confidence and brought me here. The space is too small to name them all, but I am grateful to everyone who contributed to this journey of mine.

And finally, many thanks to Notion Press for giving aspiring authors like me a platform to turn our dreams into reality.

1. A dual life

My fingers dash across the keyboard,
As lofty numbers adorn the spreadsheet.
My pen glides across the diary,
As I pour my emotions into stanzas neat.
It's a dual life I lead,
Work. Write. Sleep. Repeat.

A finance executive by the day,
Juggling with numbers during the week;
A writer by the night,
Reading Ruskin Bond and Tennyson as dusk begins to peak;
It's a dual life I lead,
Two streams flowing into my life's creek.

Tossed into the game of life,
Like a coin, its two sides;
Unaware where one side ends,
And the other begins;
It's a double role,
Like a parent raising twins.

For the personal folder on my office laptop,
Has poems typed out on an excel;

And the last pages of my diary,
Has notes, numbers and a client meeting trail.
Oh how it haunts me, this dual life of mine,
Will I ace it, or will I fail?

For while one fills my pocket,
The other fills my soul;
It's a constant tug of war,
Between what gives me stability,
And what makes me whole.

2. Aloo paratha

Dadi made the best *aloo parathas*.
She would roast the potatoes from every angle,
And I would happily listen to the jingle of her bangles,
As she baked the *paratha* into a neat triangle.

Dadi sang old songs,
While we played *antakshari* in the evening;
She celebrated every festival with utmost delight,
And joy always brimming.

Dadi had a *nuskha* for every problem I'd face;
And she taught me to be brave,
Told me there was so much out there for me to ace.

Dadi loved embroidery and crafts,
And I was her chaperone on all her trips to the weekend marts,
Where she'd buy laces, beads and all things decorative,
And I think that's how I've got an instinct slightly creative.

From homemade hair oil to homemade *achaar*,
I had everything served on a platter right within my sight,
So if you guessed I was dadi's pampered child,

Well, you are absolutely right.

When I left for college, Dadi was in tears,
'Cause while I was looking at my future,
And all the uncertainties involved,
Dadi was letting go of the kid,
Around whom her world revolved.

Two years later, Dadi fell terribly ill,
And from thereon, things just went downhill.
As she kept getting weak,
In the mundane, some happy moments we would try to sneak;
Like her stories and our naps,
But life had other plans perhaps.

Let me share an incident from her last days,
That left me awe-stricken.
When I was visiting home for holidays,
She slowly rolled her wheelchair into the kitchen.
And with trembling hands she roasted those potatoes from every angle,
And flipped the *paratha* until it made her classic neat triangle.

And right in that moment I knew-
That unconditional love,
Gives exceptional courage to you.

For ever since Dadi passed,
I've tried every *aloo paratha* I could,
But none of them have ever tasted,
The way Dadi's would.

3. Bucket list

When I was kid,
I believed in Santa and magic.
I made a list of things I wanted,
And places to be visited;
Every year, sans all logic.

By the time the myth broke,
And my rationality awoke,
I had developed a habit to keep a bucket list-
My tomorrow's little gist.

My list kept growing-
From pokemon balls to flashy brands across malls,
From chocolate bars to owning luxury cars,
From cricket set to flying in a private jet,
From Santa's sleigh to a trip to Ladakh-Leh.

While clearing some old clutter today,
I found a piece of paper dated 2001-
Wherein I had described in a handwriting quite crappy,
How a remote control car would make me happy.

I smiled and took the paper to mom.

'Ma, have a look at how stupid I was'.
'And now?' she exclaimed critically.
Puzzled, I looked at her quizzically.

'What will make you happy now?'
'Hefty paycheck and a bungalow!'
'Sure about that?'
It was time I put on my thinking hat.

'Happiness has nothing to do with the list.'
'But that's my tomorrow's gist!'
'Baby, don't fit your tomorrow into a fist.'

I looked at her, and something inside me felt a twist,
I opened my latest bucket list.
And on the top of all unexplored boxes of treasure,
Wrote: kindness, happiness, and love beyond measure.

4. Did you miss home again?

Did the twinkle in your eyes fade,
In the middle of a smile?
Did you video call your old friend,
Under the pretext that it's been a while?

Did you stare into the hollow eyes of strangers,
Searching for familiarity?
Did you sheepishly resort to music,
To bring your heart and brain at parity?

Did you drink a little too much,
And convince yourself that freedom is good?
Did you come back to an empty room at night,
And cold, half-cooked food?

Did you learn to wake up to alarms?
Did you find a way to mitigate your qualms?
Did you try putting those words on paper, but in vain?
Did you miss home again?

5. Donut

Like a donut-
My life and yours,
Sugar-coated and sparkly.
A pint of tangible ecstasy,
The sweetest fantasy.

Like a donut-
My life and yours,
With a hole in the heart;
An aching void,
The darkness within light.

6. Finding God

After a long day on the pavement,
With his back slightly bent,
The beggar crawls to the bakery,
And stares from the ground,
At the variety of breads and people;
A sight so profound.
Tired of hunger's scowl,
His stomach makes a loud growl.
The baker gives him a sandwich, a slight smile, and a nod,
And in the baker's kindness, the beggar finds his God.

A little kid breaks his neighbour's glass window again,
The old woman waddles to the window pane.
Calls at the boy to give him an earful,
The boy turns up, puppy eyes, mock tearful.
It was their ritual-
The ball hitting the window, or rolling into her garden,
The kid rushing to grab it, and to beg her pardon;
Stopping by for a few minutes to tell her about what he did at
school,
The old woman listening to him go about, while she grabbed
a stool.
The boy would mimic, laugh, and show her his antics odd,

And in his sparkling happy eyes, old granny would find her
God.

A girl is sitting in the hospital,
Imagining all scenarios possible,
With her heart in her palms,
And her mind full of qualms.
Post five hours of surgery, the doctor walks out of the
operation theater,
Her throat forms a lump, zoning out the background chatter.
'He's doing fine', the doctor says with a smile broad,
In that very hospital room, the girl finds her God.

So, let's drop that jealousy beneath the hay,
For we don't know who might need a win today,
Let's share a smile, and do our best,
Let's give someone's aching heart a rest.
For I know, someday or other,
In some way or another,
We have all been saved by someone,
From our demons and bad days.
We have all seen light, and found our Gods,
In certain people, and their kind ways.

7. Hope in the times of Corona

I fly to the nest I had left years back,
With sanitized gloves, masks, and a heavy backpack;
A backpack full of the hustle outside home,
And trailing nostalgia from a time unknown.

As the noise of the outside world fades away,
And the voice within has its say,
I find my way back to my little shots of joy-
Finish the book long left unread,
Write a poem, paint a canvas red,
Relish mornings with air fresher than before,
Beaming smiles and sunshine galore.

There are long days of being engrossed in work,
Type, call, mute, stretch, call, mail, wait... let's not go berserk!
I tumble and fumble, and indulge in some introspection of self;
Learn to go easy on people around me, and myself.
I realize there are jokes old friends can always laugh at,
No matter how much we have grown.
I decode the rocket science of preparing a meal on my own.

The world pauses and gets moving again,
As we lend each other a helping hand,
Capturing days in moments;
And moments in happy screenshots.

I sip on my *dalgona* coffee,
And browse through the news,
I choose to focus on how resilient we are.
On how, before anything else,
We must be humane;
And as long as we hold onto love and faith,
We can always hope for a better world again.

Poet's note: This poem was written during the first wave of the Coronavirus in 2020, while the world around us was changing in ways we could never have imagined.

8. I feel anxious

I walk into the room,
And forget what I had entered it for;
Like a facepalm emoji coming to life,
I slap my face and mutter a cuss word.
I feel anxious.

I'm starting afresh,
And moving ahead,
Taking compromises in my stride,
Along this bumpy ride.
And the future is so uncertain,
All conversations about it, I tend to avoid;
And the inevitable feeling that it brings,
Of being anxious.

I chalk down a plan,
I write out a to-do list,
But I'm thrown off by the reality
Of what life has to offer each day;
These plans never seem to work out my way!
Lack of execution skills? You could say.
But did destiny ever from its path, sway?
Fighting FOMO in this life so precious,

I feel anxious.

I feel my stomach clench,
And my mind race,
At a speed unknown;
Oscillating between highs and lows,
Careful caresses and merciless blows,
Trying to emerge victorious,
Over thoughts obnoxious,
I feel anxious.

9. Infinity

I splash every colour I find,
On the blank canvas left behind,
In the hope that I'll discover the hue;
That, even if slightly, resembles you.

I pen down all the words-
Obscure or relevant,
Sentences and syllables;
And yet -
The pages breathe of the same emptiness.

The emptiness that bleeds through the pages,
And seeps into our lives,
Until we see your uninhibited smile,
And the sparkle in your eyes,
Peeping from the 16*12 frame-
Hung in the heart of our home's premise.

The celebration of life is tricky,
But your parrot nose was never picky,
You danced your heart out till the last beat;
And then before we knew, you flashed a smile-
And had your final backflip.

Numb without your laughter,
And yet bursting with your myriad memories,
Our hearts wrench and swell,
While home's flooded with your colourful stories.

There's only so much a man can do,
In the numbered days that he's graced with;
And yet, with utmost beauty,
You put those numbers to shame,
And gave us our Infinity!

So, here's what I'm taking from you-
To love with an open heart,
To not be afraid of a new start,
To have a mind that never stops learning,
To put in my best at every wheel I'm turning.

I hope you're rocking the Other Life,
Like you've rocked our concert;
And I hope, while you read this,
You're having your favourite dessert.

Poet's note: This poem was written for my grandfather, after he suddenly left us for his heavenly abode.

10. Is my poetry good enough?

Everytime I pen down a poem,
A wave of exhilaration sweeps over me,
Followed by a feeling of immediate insecurity-
Is my poem good enough?

Does it lose its rhythm?
Or does it rhyme a lot?
How about a free-flowing verse in the middle?
Or maybe an inspiring thought?

Does it talk about a trending topic?
Is it relevant in the present day and time?
Does it relate to the readers' sentiments?
Is it more than just a pastime?

Is the theme too simple?
Are the sentences well constructed?
Am I communicating my feelings right?
Or am I portraying a view obstructed?

My mind swirls for a bit,
Like an unprepared kid's before a surprise test,

But I know that every word I write,
Gives me solace despite this quest.

So, I place my hand over my heart,
And fight through all these thoughts rough,
As long as it fills my soul,
My poetry will always be enough.

11. Meeting Love

I was looking for a love that sweeps me off my feet,
The kind that's the dream of every Bollywood buff,
The one with roses and surprises,
Grand proposals and all that fluff.

I was looking for a love that's loud and unafraid.
The declare-your-feelings-shouting-from-the-rooftop kinda love,
The tags-you-in-all-insta-stories kinda love,
The flaunts-you-and-treats-you-like-a-princess kinda love.

I looked for years and nothing came close.
You see, in real life, hardly anyone plans a flash mob when they propose.
So logically, I dropped this pursuit so tough,
I convinced myself that I didn't need anyone, and I was enough.

So, I was not looking when Love met me,
On a random day in October 2021.
He was very different from what I had pictured,
So it took me some time to realise that he's the one.

Love was quiet and gentle,
There was no noise around him.
With him, he brought so much peace,
He let me be myself, put my thoughts at ease.

Love didn't shout from any rooftop,
He rather whispered his feelings in my ears in the quiet of the
night.
Love never posted a single photo of us on Instagram,
But he applauded my LinkedIn achievements with all his
might.

Love was no knight in shining armour,
So he didn't treat me like a damsel in distress.
Love treated me like an equal,
Like a best friend, not some glorified princess.

Love didn't flaunt any feelings in public.
He didn't need to.
Together, we built a tiny world of our own,
With inside jokes and secrets and companionship;
That with each day, in its abundance, grew.

Love was not so big on planning surprises,
So, Love gave me a happy home to walk into.
Love built a safe space for me,
To run into, crash into, fall into.

Love opened his arms to me,
After every tiring day, to rush into.

It's been quite some time since I've known Love,
And for him, I can't ever thank my stars enough.
Love is my support, my cheerleader;
The one whose lame jokes throw me into a laughing fit.
So that's my story of meeting Love,
And I'd never trade it for any box office hit.

12. Not like other girls

Growing up,
I let the statement 'Not like other girls',
Masquerade as a compliment;
Call it a lack of self-awareness,
Or an urge to be different.

But "like other girls",
I'm equally motivated, and exhausted,
For new clothes and earrings, I'm equally excited,
I've also got my heart broken, yet wear it on my sleeve;
I also crush on fictional men,
And some unattainable fantasies, I let myself weave.

"Like other girls",
I'm fighting for my voice to be heard in every meeting,
I'm dealing with period cramps, and going about life, like it's nothing.
I'm trying to find the balance between being practical and being emotional,
I'm teaching myself that it's okay to be vulnerable.

"Like other girls",
I'm trying to be assertive, yet not aggressive,

I'm trying to let go of years of mental conditioning, and thoughts regressive,
I'm trying to be the ideal daughter and daughter-in-law,
Between self care and selfishness, I'm looking for a line to draw.

"Like other girls",
I'm learning to stand up for myself,
I'm learning that it's okay to ask for help.
I'm learning that no-one can do it all,
That superwoman is a myth, just a poster in the mall.

So, if you want to compliment me next,
Let me tell you what works best.
Tell me that I'm brave and strong,
Tell me that it's okay even if I go wrong,
Tell me I'm enough the way I am,
Tell me that perfection is just another scam.
Let me dance through life, create my own twirls,
Tell me that I'm "like other girls".

13. Not yet

Before I begin,
I'd like to ask,
Are you living your dream life,
Or hiding behind a mask?
Have you kept your real goals on hold,
To be pursued, after you finish this 'important task'?

Are you waiting for the right time,
Or the right balance in your bank?
Are you waiting for an easy week at work,
Or the day when your body has a full energy tank?
Are you waiting for things to fall in line,
So that you don't waste your time filling the blank?

I hope you tell me that this is the life
You've always wanted,
I hope for fruits,
In every seed you've planted.

But if you didn't apply for the job,
That you aspired for,
As you thought,
You didn't have in you

What they desired for;

Then, let me tell you, you're not alone.

Give it a shot,

For good things happen outside the comfort zone.

Let me urge you to do a little reset,

And let go of the "Not yet".

14. One love

A trillion hellos in one life;
Concealed blushes, stolen glances.

A billion goodbyes in one life;
Hidden tears, fake smiles.

A million people in one life;
Escalated heartbeats, passive formalities.

A thousand moments in one life;
Ecstatic highs, pit-bottom lows.

A hundred lies in one life;
Distorted truths, masked faces.

A familiar person, for the entire life;
Two cups of coffee, a blanket, and stars.

15. Permanent song

I brew an espresso,

And pick up 'The perks of being a wallflower'

From my bookshelf.

I know that we accept the love we think we deserve,

I know the plot verb by verb,

But,

Don't we all reread our favourite lines,

From our favourite books,

A thousand times over?

The moon's shining bright tonight,

The clock's inching midnight,

A faint jingle plays on the radio;

And I wonder how,

When some songs are released,

One of them strikes a chord in our hearts.

We keep listening to it,

Over and over again,

Day and night, on a loop.

But how the ecstasy is fast fleeting,

How we witness the thrill retreating,

And it is replaced as soon as another song comes up;

Of how easy it is to replace-

Some songs and some people,
And how desperately we hold onto some.

For there's this one song that knocks at our soul,
The one we listen to at 2:30 a.m. in the night,
When things are quiet and dark,
Or at 2:30 p.m. in the day,
When things seem to be falling apart.
This song is our savior,
This is the song that rights every wrong,
This is our permanent song.

16. Peter Pan

Rainy days are a brewing pot for nostalgia,
For fragments of memory,
Flashing across like everyday trivia.

Rain brings lots of memories for me,
But the oldest is from when I was three.
I sat by the window in Papa's office,
And it's been years,
So pardon me if I don't recollect the entire premise.

What I do remember is a story Papa told me.
That of Peter Pan,
The boy who never grew up, the resident of Neverland.

I loved stories, and imagined a tiny boy,
Flying across the wonder land. Oh, such joy!
I looked outside the window,
At the black electric and telephone wires,
Getting drenched in the pouring rain,
And from them, hung little water droplets,
Neatly in a line, like bogies of a train.

Papa was sitting in a chair,

Was it revolving? I don't remember.
He was fiddling with the green paperweight,
Which, as I call to mind,
Has been his cabin's permanent member.
It was the rain, tiny water droplets, Papa and me-
Our small world, that office chamber.

After that day, I've often wondered about Peter Pan,
So cool to not grow up, such magic!
What a shame to lose out on the adult world's charm, how
tragic!

And every time it rains,
I still think of Peter Pan's story,
Of how the most random things,
Can jog our most distant memory.

I wonder how we are all made of tales,
We heard as a kid,
And how much impact those stories have,
In spreading happiness across our life's grid.
Do all grown-ups still take shelter in their happy memories,
Flying past their marvel, just like Peter Pan did?

17. Promise?

If I told you you're beautiful,
Would you believe me,
Or would you laugh it off,
Like it's too hard to see?

If I told you you're perfect,
Would you bet on that,
Or would you think of how clumsily you dropped your drink,
Yesterday night, in your colleague's flat?

If I told you, you light up the room,
Would your face shine bright,
Or would you shyly look away,
Not trusting your own light?

If I told you I love the way you sing,
Would you sing aloud and sway,
Or would you go back to the school music competition,
When you forgot your song on the final day?

If I told you I liked your jacket,
Would you swell an inch with grace,
Or would you try to hide your extra tummy fat,

You can't seem to erase?

If I told you, you have immense potential,
That your achievements so far are just a trailer,
Would you try harder for your goals,
Or would you fall prey to your last failure?

And if I told you joy is handy,
Would you smile for me,
Or with me, Or at me,
For I don't care about the preposition,
As long as you're smiling.

For I might then go on to tell you,
That love is possible, and so is living;
Like those crazy idiots,
Who are not embarrassed at all, of losing bets or going wrong,
Like those friends who fill in, when one of them forgets the
song.

So promise me,
Every time I tell you, 'You can do it',
You will let go of all your self doubts and insecurities,
And run with open arms to chase your dreams.
And everytime I tell you that happiness comes easy,
You will not wonder whether it's meant to be or not,
Promise me, you will give it a shot.

18. Search for Peace

I sat in a meditation centre,
My eyes shut, focussing hard.
I tried to listen to the hymn chants;
And within some obscure minutes,
My mind began its random rants.

I sat alone in a balcony,
Overlooking the forest;
And heard the crickets sing.
And just when I thought I had cracked the code,
My cell phone went *ping*!

I went to temples and churches,
I spent my evenings on several beaches.
I looked for Peace on hill-tops,
In soothing songs, sunsets, and pouring rain;
But it somehow kept slipping, again and again.

So gradually the quest lost its poise,
I became a part of all the traffic and noise.
Until, on a leisure trip,
I decided to stop running and pause for a bit.
Switched off my phone, picked up a book;

And there Peace was, smirking.
Directly into my eyes, Peace shot a funny look-
'You searched for me beyond reason and rhyme,
While I was within you, all this time!'

19. Seasonal love

Like winter, with all its grace;
He walks into your life.
Brightly, you smile and shine,
Like fresh, gleaming snow.

Like spring, with all its vigour;
He lights up your life.
Ecstatic, you dance and roll,
Like a garden in full bloom.

Like summer, he heats things up;
Ice melts, sparks fly.
Crazily, you trip and toss,
Like giving up control.

Like autumn, he waves a goodbye,
Crisp and sunburnt.
Dizzily, you slip and fall,
Like a leaf losing its home.

20. She is everything

Her boss needs a critical update,
She needs to hurry.
Her cook is calling out of the kitchen,
Asking what *masalas* to use in today's curry.
With her laptop in one hand,
And coriander powder in the other,
She tries to manage both the duties,
The woman is a juggler.

She makes *rangolis* in every corner of her house,
She laughs for photos with her whole family,
Her wedding is fixed and she's soon going to be
Someone else's *Ghar ki Lakshmi;*
It's her last *Maayke wali Diwali.*
She hides her emotions beneath a smile;
Despite her woes, she knows how to paint a happy picture,
The woman is a painter.

She cooks dinner for her kids,
While running a 102-degree fever.
She challenges the status quo in meeting rooms,
Without her confidence showing the slightest quiver.
While sailing everyone across the ocean,

She loses herself at the bay,
But she doesn't let her individuality sway;
She defies her self-doubt everyday.
The woman is a warrior.

She's the puppy eyes asking her husband for extra cuddles,
She's the strong arms holding him through all his struggles.
She's the bossy sister teaching her younger brother MS Excel tricks,
She's the vulnerable teenager, PMSing and crying over ice cream sticks.
The woman is a rainbow of emotions,
Making a full red to violet swing,
The woman is a paradox,
She is everything.

21. Silence, please?

Seven months back, was the first time we had met;
In a library, between two books by Coelho, neatly set.
I had stolen glances, while you smiled directly at me,
We were both on a reading spree.

Six days of smiling at each other, and I knew it was time,
I got my speakers ready, but you were heading for a mime.
So, I played along;
Life had taught me good things often took a time too long.

Five weeks passed by like a super smooth ride,
I read more than I had ever done in my life-
From genres earlier unexplored,
To the older editions that the library stored.

Four days back, I pumped up my courage so tame,
And went to the librarian, who by now, knew me by my first
name.
Like a routine, you joined me in the line,
And now, I was not going to waste any time.

Three seconds of thoughts so quick,

After which I turned and asked 'Hey, which book did you pick'?
You smiled and just stared at me with those brown eyes,
Embarrassed, I realised it was a step unwise.

Two readers later, came my turn,
I got the books issued, and was ready for a run,
To redeem myself of how stupid I felt,
A situation with which I had rarely dealt.

One minute of delay in the printing of my receipt,
Your turn came, and I felt a pang of deceit;
Until the librarian smiled at you, and stamped your book's first page,
And you thanked her in sign language!

22. Solace

She revels in the little joys of life,
And bombards me with non-stop optimism;
She wraps me in multiple layers of care,
And turns my woes into joyous rainbows-
Through her magic prism.

She defeats me in card games,
And calls my friends by nicknames;
She's savage, and laughs at lame videos,
She's mastered the art of differentiating-
Between my real friends and foes.

Courage is her middle name,
And we have seen her face everything upfront,
She is our rock, our daily dose of happiness;
And only a plate of hot samosas seems to be her weakness!

She makes sure our tummies are full,
Our beds are warm, and our lives bright.
She never gets tired of looking out for us,
No matter how far we are from her sight.

She has built our lives, on sacrifices innumerable,

On lessons, lullabies, scoldings, and her real-life heroic fable,
Through her, I've known how to love beyond condition,
And that love is life's true definition.

We argue a lot,
Disagree at almost every phase,
But when nothing seems to work,
In her smile, I find my solace.

Poet's note: This poem is for the one who holds our home, and our lives together- my mother.

23. Something borrowed

The little kid's dad buys him a bunch of balloons,
With an uninhibited laugh,
He lets the wind sway those balloons away;
Can I borrow that laugh for a day?

The boatman is rowing his boat as dusk falls,
Enjoying a quiet sunset.
These moments of quiet and peace,
Can I borrow for myself, please?

The small town girl toils day and night,
To fulfill for her parents,
The dreams and hopes they left behind.
Can I borrow her ambition, her grind?

The golden retriever wags its tail,
Catches the ball, and runs back to the man,
Whose loneliness disappears every time the dog is around.
Can I borrow this love unbound?

For when the time comes,
I will give it back with interest,
The laughs and love and hope,

That I've borrowed from people along the way;

For despite our differences,

We're all looking for a place to belong to,

For some peace, and the strength to keep our sorrows at bay;

We're all living on borrowed lessons and moments,

Hoping that on the day of the final tally,

We would have borrowed some good,

And given some more away.

24. Sunflower

The petals unfurl,
Smitten, baby bee does a tiny twirl.
Droplets of sunshine kiss me slow,
And I let the breeze give me a lazy blow.

You illuminate my world-
My soul, you ignite,
And yet so modestly,
Take to the background,
And let me steal the limelight.

Piercing rays of joy through my gloom,
You watch over me, as I bloom;
Like a parent, like a lover,
Like Sun to a Sunflower.

25. Way back home

You're the sound of temple bells on a Tuesday morning,
You're the clanking of utensils in the kitchen,
You're the *Sarabhai Vs Sarabhai* on a lazy evening,
You're the *poha* in breakfast with extra *dhaniya*,
You're the strong *adrak wali chai*,
You're the train chugging into the platform of my town,
You're mom's chiding when I wake up super late on the weekend,
You're dad's reminder for making my investments on time,
You're the feeling of knowing who's coming by the sound of footsteps,
You're the smell of petrichor after a long dry summer,
You're my hiding corner,
You're my echo point,
You're my rhyming poem,
You're my way back home.

Legacy

Writing came as a legacy to me. My grandfather (Late Shri Mukutdhari Agrawal), among other things, was an eloquent writer and a compelling orator. He passed on the love for writing and oratory to my father and aunts, who in turn passed it down to me and my brother. Many people, who have known my family, and seen me write or perform, have said, '*Yeh toh iske khoon mein hai,* It's in her blood.' And I agree. I'm so grateful and privileged to have this legacy to carry forward with me.

Dadaji and Dadi, you're always in our memories. May you be at peace wherever you are.

My lovely readers- I hope you had a good time reading *Apricity & Stardust,* and that you get to read more from me in the future. You can follow me on Instagram @ chime_and_rhyme (Sakshi Agrawal).